HENRY *Clay*

SPIRIT
of America®

HENRY *Clay*

THE GREAT COMPROMISER

By Michael Burgan

Content Adviser: Eric Brooks, Curator, Ashland, the Henry Clay Estate,
Lexington, Kentucky

The Child's World®
Chanhassen, Minnesota

9

HENRY *Clay*

Published in the United States of America by The Child's World®
PO Box 326 • Chanhassen, MN 55317-0326 • 800-599-READ • www.childsworld.com

Acknowledgments
The Child's World®: Mary Berendes, Publishing Director

Editorial Directions, Inc.: E. Russell Primm, Editorial Director; Pam Rosenberg, Line Editor; Katie Marsico, Assistant Editor; Matthew Messbarger, Editorial Assistant; Susan Hindman, Copy Editor; Susan Ashley, Proofreader; Julie Zaveloff, Chris Simms, and Peter Garnham, Fact Checkers; Tim Griffin/IndexServ, Indexer; Dawn Friedman, Photo Researcher; Linda S. Koutris, Photo Selector

The Design Lab: Kathleen Petelinsek, Art Direction; Kari Thornborough, Page Production

Photo
Cover: Bettmann/Corbis; Bettmann/Corbis: 2, 10, 11, 14, 17, 24, 25; Corbis: 15, 23; The Filson Historical Society, Louisville, Kentucky: 7; The Granger Collection, New York: 6, 18, 19; Hulton|Archive/Getty Images: 27; Library of Congress: 9; North Wind Picture Archives: 13, 20; Stock Montage, Inc.: 28.

Library of Congress Cataloging-in-Publication Data
Burgan, Michael.
  Henry Clay : the Great Compromiser / by Michael Burgan.
    v. cm.— (Our people)
  Includes bibliographical references and index.
  Contents: Young lawyer and politician—Leader of the House—Presidential politics—Last years in Washington.
  ISBN 1-59296-174-6 (Lib. bdg. : alk. paper)
  1. Clay, Henry, 1777–1852—Juvenile literature. 2. Legislators—United States—Biography—Juvenile literature. 3. United States. Congress. Senate—Biography—Juvenile literature. 4. United States—Politics and government—1815–1861—Juvenile literature. [1. Clay, Henry, 1777–1852. 2. Statesmen. 3. Legislators. 4. United States—Politics and government—1815–1861.] I. Title. II. Series.
  E340.C6 B87 2004
  973.5'092—dc22d   2003018120

14 20 25

Contents

Chapter ONE

Young Lawyer and Politician

Henry Clay is remembered for his political service at a time when America was developing as a nation. Although not everyone agreed with Clay's political views while he was alive, after his death several historians honored him by saying he was among the greatest U.S. senators ever.

IN THE FIRST HALF OF THE 19TH CENTURY, THE United States faced many difficult issues. During that time, Henry Clay played a large role in helping the country meet those challenges. He served in both the U.S. House of Representatives and the U.S. Senate, and he also ran for president several times. Clay is best known for promoting what he called the American System. He believed the U.S. government should try to create a strong national economy.

Many people did not share Clay's views on the American System. They opposed having the government play an active role in the economy. Clay always argued strongly for his beliefs. Yet he also tried to reach a **compromise** if he thought political arguments might hurt the country. Clay was often called the Great Compromiser.

Henry Clay was born on April 12, 1777, in Hanover County, Virginia. His father, John, was a minister and a tobacco farmer. Clay's mother, Elizabeth, was the daughter of a wealthy plantation owner. As a boy, Henry attended a oneroom schoolhouse with a dirt floor. Later in life, he admitted he had not studied as hard as he should have. Still, he had great intelligence,

Interesting Fact

▶ When Clay was born, the American Revolution was under way. The United States was fighting for independence from Great Britain. British soldiers once stormed through Clay's home, searching for valuables to steal. Clay remembered this incident the rest of his life.

Henry Clay was born in this house in Hanover County, Virginia.

which helped him succeed during his career. He also had an early interest in public speaking. His speaking skills helped him when he ran for public office.

Clay's father died during the American Revolution, and his mother remarried. In 1791, she and her new husband moved to Kentucky, but they left Henry in Virginia to continue his education. He began studying law, and in 1797, he received a license to work as a lawyer. Soon after, he left for Kentucky. Within a few months, Clay was practicing law in Lexington.

On April 11, 1799, he married Lucretia Hart. She came from one of the wealthiest families in Lexington. She devoted herself to taking care of the Clay home and raising a family. The Clays eventually had 11 children. Several of them died while they were still young.

Clay did well as a lawyer. His business grew, and he earned enough money to buy large pieces of land. He also became interested in politics and supported the Republican Party.

In 1803, Clay won a seat in the Kentucky legislature, the branch of government that makes laws. He supported laws that strengthened banks and **commerce.** Some Republicans opposed these measures. They thought the laws favored wealthy people over the interests of average working people. Clay believed, however, that the govern-

ment should help businesses grow. In the end, all citizens would benefit, not just the rich.

In 1806, Kentucky lawmakers chose Clay to serve briefly as one of the state's two U.S. senators. He filled in for the previous senator, who had resigned. In Washington, D.C., Clay met many important political leaders. He also impressed people with his speaking skills.

Henry Clay named his home in Lexington "Ash Land" because of the large number of ash trees located on the property. Today, Ashland is open to the public and gives visitors a look at the home where Clay lived from 1806 until 1852.

9

After America won its independence in 1783, many of the country's leaders hoped there would not be political parties. They believed parties created conflict that made it hard to run a government. But people who shared similar ideas on important issues wanted to work together. And because not everyone had the same ideas about what was best for the United States, political parties did form. People with similar ideas joined the same party.

The Republican Party was founded by Thomas Jefferson (left) during the 1790s. Jefferson had written the Declaration of Independence, and in 1800 he was elected the third U.S. president. The members of his party were sometimes called Jeffersonian Republicans or Democratic Republicans. The Republicans believed each state should have as much freedom as possible to run its own affairs. Most party members thought the country should acquire new lands in the West whenever it could. Republicans also supported farmers and their economic interests. By the time Henry Clay entered the Senate, however, some Republicans were calling for laws that would help manufacturers.

The other major party at the time was the Federalist Party. Its first leader was Alexander Hamilton (right). He served as the first secretary of the treasury. Hamilton wanted a strong national government. Federalists also called for close ties with Great Britain. Most Republicans did not trust the British. They believed Great Britain wanted to limit U.S. trade with other nations.

Leader of the House

▶ In 1809, Clay fought a duel with another Kentucky lawmaker. The two men fired pistols at each other, and each received a slight wound. Clay fought another duel in 1826 against John Randolph, one of his political rivals in Congress. Neither one was injured.

BY THE FALL OF 1807, CLAY WAS BACK IN THE Kentucky legislature. Three years later, he returned to Washington, once again to complete the term of a Kentucky senator. In 1811, he won an election to serve in the U.S. House of Representatives.

At the time, the United States was inching close to a war with Great Britain. The British had been fighting the French since the 1790s. During that long war, the United States had remained neutral, choosing not to help either side. Americans continued to trade with both nations. The British, however, tried to limit U.S. trade with France. Also, British ships sometimes stopped American vessels to search for sailors who had deserted the British navy. At times, American sailors were wrongly accused of being British citizens. The British would take those Americans and force them to work for the British, a practice known as impressment.

Starting in the early 1800s, U.S. leaders demanded that the British stop impressing sailors and limiting U.S. trade. The British refused. By 1811, Clay and many other Republicans wanted a war with Great Britain, to force them to end their policies. These lawmakers were called the War Hawks, and Clay was their leader. In December 1811, he wrote, "War . . . seems to me the only alternative worthy of our Country." The War Hawks also hoped the United States could take control of British lands in Canada if a war was fought with Great Britain.

As war neared, the Republicans dominated the U.S. government. The president, James Madison,

Before the American Revolution, the British navy would sometimes send "press gangs" ashore in the colonies in search of sailors. After the war, press gangs no longer set foot on American land, but they still stopped ships at sea.

The British set fire to the White House in 1814, during the War of 1812. First Lady Dolley Madison is remembered for her bravery and quick thinking during this attack. Before leaving the White House, she saved artist Gilbert Stuart's famous portrait of George Washington.

was a Republican and the party controlled Congress. In 1812, Republicans in the House of Representatives chose Clay as the Speaker of the House. This is the most important position in the House. Up until then, however, speakers had not always played a powerful role in the House of Representatives. Clay changed that. He chose representatives who shared his views to lead **committees.** These committees did much of the actual work in the House. They shaped proposed laws, known as bills. Clay also asserted his right to take part in debates and vote on bills. Past speakers hadn't used that right. Clay was determined to be a strong leader for his party.

Clay worked closely with President Madison to make sure Congress declared war on Great Britain. The war, however, did not go well for the Americans. Several invasions of Canada failed. Later in the war, British troops invaded Washington, D.C., and burned down the White House. By 1814, the U.S. government was almost out of money. At the end of that year, the Americans and British sent **diplomats** to Belgium to discuss ending the war. Clay was one of the diplomats representing the United States.

When the war ended, Clay was still Speaker of the House. He pushed his plan to build new roads and canals and help manufacturers. Even though he was a Republican, Clay was a nationalist—he wanted a strong national government and economy. He was willing to limit some of the power held by state governments if he could improve the lives of all Americans. Clay called the policies he supported the American System.

As part of his program, Clay wanted tariffs—taxes placed on foreign goods brought into the United States. Tariffs helped the government raise money. They also helped American businesses. The tariffs raised the price of foreign goods. As the price of foreign goods rose,

The Treaty of Ghent officially ended the War of 1812. Four other U.S. diplomats besides Clay attended the signing of the treaty—U.S. ambassador Jonathan Russell, future president John Quincy Adams, Delaware senator Ashton Bayard, and former secretary of the U.S. treasury Albert Gallatin.

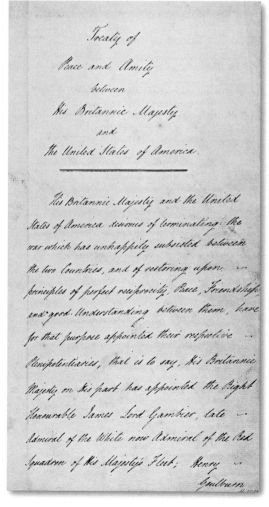

15

Americans bought more U.S. goods, since they were cheaper. The U.S. companies that made those goods earned more money and hired more people to work for them.

Clay also backed a national bank. The government had first created one in 1791, but it had stopped operating in 1811. In 1816, Clay worked to reopen the Bank of the United States. Both private **investors** and the government owned part of the national bank.

Clay also worked on issues not related to the American System. The most important was the spread of slavery. In 1819, the territory of Missouri was hoping to enter the Union as a state. Slavery was legal in the territory. Some members of Congress, however, wanted to put limits on slavery in Missouri when it became a state. They also called for slowly freeing the existing slaves there. As a result, there would eventually be no slaves in Missouri. The lawmakers who proposed limiting slavery were from the North. In the Northern states, slavery was already illegal or was gradually ending. Southern states, however, still supported slavery. Their members of Congress fought the effort to end slavery in Missouri.

Clay had mixed feelings about slavery. On his farm, he owned slaves. He believed he needed them to keep the farm running. He had grown up in a region that considered slavery a normal part of life. Yet Clay also believed that slavery was harmful to

both the slaves and the nation. He hoped it would slowly end across the country. Clay once wrote that if he lived in a state where slavery didn't exist, "I would certainly oppose its introduction with all the force and energy in my power." But Clay believed the decision to allow or prevent slavery was up to each state, not the national government.

At first, Clay opposed the efforts to limit slavery in Missouri. Then, as Congress debated the issue, he began to change his mind. He saw that Northerners wanted the bill and Southerners opposed it. Clay worried that the split feelings over the issue might lead to a civil war, North against South. Early in

Plantation owners used slaves to perform the hard work of picking cotton. While Clay had mixed feelings about slavery, he did believe in a movement that aimed to resettle freed slaves in the African country of Liberia.

1820, he made a series of powerful speeches that called for a compromise.

At the time, Maine was also trying to enter the Union as a state. Slavery was not allowed there, and some Southerners opposed letting Maine enter the Union. Clay and others supported a bill that would let Missouri enter as a slave state and Maine enter as a free state. In addition, slavery would be limited in new states in the West. Only states located south of a line that started at Missouri's southern border could have slaves. Congress accepted this "Missouri Compromise," and Clay earned his nickname, the Great Compromiser.

This map reflects the terms of the Missouri Compromise of 1820. Thanks to Clay's political skills, the issue of slavery in new U.S. territories remained somewhat settled for more than 30 years. Unfortunately, his fear of a civil war became a reality in 1861.

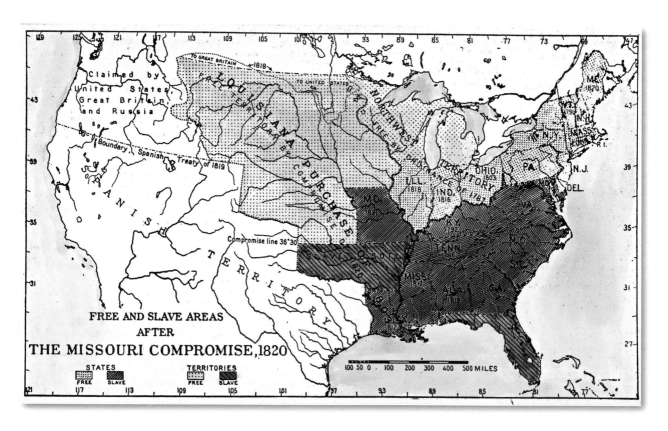

FREE AND SLAVE AREAS
AFTER
THE MISSOURI COMPROMISE, 1820

NOT ALL AMERICANS WANTED TO FIGHT THE WAR OF 1812. FEDERALISTS strongly opposed the war, because they wanted good relations with Great Britain. Some New England Federalists were so upset about the war, they talked about breaking off from the United States and forming their own government, but they never did.

For the United States, the best moments of the war came at sea. The U.S.S. *Constitution* destroyed a British warship in August 1812, and it won several other battles during the war. The *Constitution* won the nickname Old Ironsides. British cannonballs seemed to bounce off the wooden ship as if it were made of iron. The U.S. Navy won another key victory on Lake Erie in 1813.

The Americans' greatest land victory came in January 1815, at the Battle of New Orleans. Andrew Jackson, a future U.S. president, was the hero there. The battle, however, would not have been fought at all if faster communications had been available at the time. The British and the Americans had signed a peace treaty a few weeks earlier, but the news did not reach the United States until after the Battle of New Orleans.

Chapter THREE

Presidential Politics

John Quincy Adams was the son of John Adams, the second U.S. president. Both men were strongly opposed to slavery.

DURING MOST OF CLAY'S YEARS AS SPEAKER OF THE House, the United States had only one major political party. The Federalists had faded out, leaving the Republicans in charge. Over time, however, members of that party began to disagree on key issues, such as slavery and the American System. In 1824, four different members of the party ran for president. Clay was one of them. The other three were John Quincy Adams, Andrew Jackson, and William Crawford.

Clay thought he had a good chance to win because he had served so long as speaker. Many political leaders, however, didn't like his American System. They also disliked him personally. In his speeches, Clay could be mean to his political opponents. And some representatives believed he sometimes did what was best for his political career, not the party or the country.

Jackson won more **electoral votes** than the other three candidates, but not enough to become president. By law, the race had to be decided in the House of Representatives. Clay had received the fewest electoral votes, so he had to drop out of the election. He still had a role to play, however, because of his job as speaker. He could use the power of that position to convince other representatives to support the person he wanted to win.

Adams and Clay were not friendly with each other, but Clay decided he preferred Adams as president over Jackson. (Crawford wasn't a likely president because of health problems.) With Clay's support, Adams won the presidency. Clay's opponents claimed that the two men had made a secret bargain. They said Adams had agreed to make Clay the next secretary of state if Clay supported him. Both men denied the charge, though Adams did make Clay his secretary of state. Jackson's supporters spoke bitterly against Clay and Adams for years to come.

As secretary of state, Clay tried to promote good relations between the United States and the countries of Central and South America. He also tried to end an old disagreement with Great Britain over trade with British colonies in the Caribbean. Clay's efforts with the British failed.

Since 1789, only two presidential elections have been decided in the House of Representatives. The first was in 1800, when Thomas Jefferson defeated Aaron Burr.

21

▸ The secretary of
state is considered the
most important mem-
ber of the president's
cabinet. The mem-
bers of the cabinet
run different govern-
ment agencies and
advise the president.
The secretary of state
helps the president
carry out foreign
affairs. During Clay's
lifetime, five men who
held that position
later served as presi-
dent: Thomas Jeffer-
son, James Madison,
James Monroe, John
Quincy Adams, and
Martin Van Buren.

In 1828, Adams ran for reelection against
Jackson. The Republicans were now known as the
National Republicans. Jackson's branch of the party
was called the Democratic Republicans. This time,
Jackson easily won the election. Clay despised Jack-
son, and he was disappointed when Adams lost.

In March 1829, Clay returned to Kentucky
to practice law, but in his heart he wanted to be
back in Washington. He got the chance in 1831,
when he was elected to the U.S. Senate. The next
year, he was named the National Republican Party's
presidential candidate. He ran against President
Jackson, whose party members were now known
simply as Democrats.

An important issue in the campaign was the
Bank of the United States. By law, the bank was
due to close. Congress passed a bill to keep the bank
open, but Jackson did not approve it. Clay said
Jackson had hurt the country by shutting the bank.
In the end, however, most American voters favored
Jackson, and he easily won the election. Clay believed his loss was bad for the country's future. He
wrote, "Whether we shall ever see . . . law and liberty
again, is very questionable."

In the Senate, Clay continued to attack Jackson
and his policies. Over the next few years, Clay
emerged as the leader of the Whigs. This new party
replaced the National Republicans as the main chal-
lenger to the Democrats. The Whigs wanted to

strengthen the American System, which the Democrats had been trying to take apart. Clay and the Whigs also wanted to weaken the power of the president. Clay believed Jackson and the Democratic president after him, Martin Van Buren, had tried to use powers that legally belonged to Congress.

Clay hoped to run as the Whig candidate for president in 1840. Once again, people within his party opposed him. He angered some Southerners when he said slavery had to end. But he also said slavery should not end right away, which upset some

Many Americans considered Andrew Jackson a representative of the common man. He had less formal schooling than several of his political enemies, but was looked upon as a hero for his bravery and military leadership.

Northerners who wanted to end it. A friend told Clay he would lose support because of his beliefs on slavery. Clay replied, "I had rather be right than be president."

The Whig candidate, William Henry Harrison, won the 1840 election. He died soon after taking office and was replaced by Vice President John Tyler. Clay was now the most important Whig in the Senate. He even challenged the president and his plans. Once Clay shouted, "Tyler dares not resist. I will drive him before me." Some senators called Clay "the Dictator," and he angered many people with his demanding ways.

Henry Clay may have been nicknamed "the Dictator," but John Tyler (right) was referred to as "His Accidency" because he became president when William Henry Harrison died in office. Tyler and Clay engaged in many bitter political struggles.

24

AFTER LOSING THE 1832 PRESIDENTIAL ELECTION, CLAY RETURNED TO HIS duties in the Senate. The country faced a difficult issue because of a tariff law passed in 1832. Leaders in South Carolina thought the law favored Northern manufacturers and hurt their state's farmers. The farmers had to pay higher prices for their goods at a time when they were making less money from the cotton they raised. The South Carolinians began to argue that the state could nullify the tariff, or declare that it was not a valid law. President Jackson said no state had the right to nullify a federal law.

By the end of 1832, South Carolina lawmakers did nullify the law. They also threatened to secede, or leave the Union, if Jackson tried to enforce it. Jackson responded by preparing troops to march into South Carolina.

Clay feared that the tariff and nullification could lead to a war. He proposed changing the tariff law. The tax rates would stay the same for nine years, then they would be cut. During that time, U.S. manufacturers could become stronger and learn how to produce goods at a lower price. Both the manufacturers and South Carolina accepted the plan. Clay said the day Congress accepted the Compromise Tariff "was the most proud and triumphant day of my life."

Last Years in Washington

▶ During the 1820s, American settlers began arriving in Texas. At the time, Texas was part of Mexico. In 1836, Texans fought a revolution to win their independence from Mexico.

HEALTH PROBLEMS FORCED HENRY CLAY TO LEAVE the Senate in 1842, but he still had his eye on the presidency. In 1844, the Whigs chose him as their presidential candidate. Slavery was an important issue during the election. So was Texas. At the time, Texas was an independent country. In 1844, some Americans wanted the United States to annex Texas, or take it into the Union so it could become a state. Others opposed this, however, because Texas had a large slave population.

At first, Clay opposed annexing Texas. As the campaign went on, however, he came out in favor of it. He sought the support of Southerners, who wanted Texas to enter the Union as a slave state. His new position upset people who opposed slavery. Clay's foes—both Democrats and **abolitionists**— spread vicious rumors about him. One opponent accused Clay of being a "common drunkard . . . thief, robber . . . and murderer." The abolitionists claimed he abused his slaves and wanted to make white people slaves as well. Clay said his opponents were using "devilish means" to defeat him, but the attacks worked. Democrat James K. Polk won the presidential election.

In 1848, Clay once again tried to be the Whig Party's candidate for president. This time he lost, as the party had moved to a stronger antislavery position. Some Whigs also thought that Clay had lost popularity and could not win the election. The next year, Clay returned to the Senate. The spread of slavery was now the most difficult issue the country faced.

A Whig banner urges supporting Clay for president. Early on, several people thought that Clay would easily win the 1844 election, but his views on slavery and the annexation of Texas cost him too many votes. Some historians believe this third unsuccessful presidential election was the most disappointing for him.

Clay died in 1852 as a result of tuberculosis, a disease that affects a person's lungs. Although he was already ill in late 1851, Clay still left his estate in Lexington, Kentucky, to attend a meeting of the U.S. Senate.

In 1846, the United States had gone to war with Mexico. After winning the war in 1848, the United States acquired land from Mexico, including California and a large part of the Southwest. Once again, as in 1820, Southerners argued that new states should be allowed to have slavery if they wanted. And once again, Clay called for a compromise. Even more than in 1820, he feared the Union might split apart if the two sides could not agree on what to do.

Clay worked for several laws that tried to address the concerns of both Northerners and Southerners. Together, these laws are known as the Compromise of 1850. In the compromise, California entered the Union as a free state. Later, other new states formed in the region could decide whether or not to allow slavery. In addition, the compromise ended the slave trade in Washington, D.C. It also made it easier for slave owners to get back slaves who ran away.

The Compromise of 1850 was Clay's last great political act. The next year, old age and bad health forced him to retire from the Senate. He died in Washington, D.C., on June 29, 1852. During his life, Clay had worked hard to strengthen the United States. He fought to solve problems that threatened to tear it apart. The Union, he once said, was "the key to my heart."

1777 Henry Clay is born on April 12, in Hanover County, Virginia.

1792 Clay begins studying law with George Wythe.

1797 Clay receives his license to practice law and moves to Lexington, Kentucky.

1799 Clay marries Lucretia Hart.

1803 Clay is elected to the Kentucky legislature.

1806 Clay serves in the U.S. Senate from November until March 1807.

1811 Clay is elected to the U.S. House of Representatives.

1812 The members of the House of Representatives choose Clay to serve as Speaker of the House.

1814 Clay signs the treaty that ends the War of 1812.

1820 Clay leads the effort to pass the Missouri Compromise.

1824 Clay loses the presidential election to John Quincy Adams; next year, Adams chooses Clay as his secretary of state.

1831 Clay returns to the U.S. Senate.

1832 Andrew Jackson easily defeats Clay for the U.S. presidency.

1840 Clay emerges as the most powerful member of the Whig Party in Congress.

1844 Clay runs for president a third time and loses to James K. Polk.

1850 Once again in the U.S. Senate, Clay pushes for the Compromise of 1850 so the issue of slavery will not divide the country.

1852 Clay dies on June 29 in Washington, D.C.

abolitionists (ab-uh-LISH-uh-nists)
During the 19th century, abolitionists were people who wanted to end slavery immediately. Abolitionists claimed Henry Clay abused his slaves.

cabinet (KAB-in-it)
A cabinet is a group of advisers who assist a president or other head of state in making decisions about how to govern a country. Henry Clay was one of the members of the cabinet during the presidency of John Quincy Adams.

commerce (KOM-urss)
Commerce is buying and selling goods to make money. Henry Clay supported laws that promoted banks and commerce.

committees (kuh-MIT-eez)
Committees are small groups of people who work together on specific issues. Clay chose representatives who shared his views to lead committees.

compromise (KOM-pruh-mize)
A compromise is an agreement in which both sides give up something they want in order to make a deal. Clay would try to reach a compromise if he thought political arguments might hurt the country.

diplomats (DIP-luh-mats)
Diplomats represent their governments in foreign countries. As a U.S. diplomat, Clay signed the treaty that ended the War of 1812 with Great Britain.

electoral votes (i-LEK-tur-uhl VOHTS)
In the United States, electoral votes are counted to see who has been elected president. Each state has the same number of electoral votes as the number of representatives it sends to Congress.

investors (in-VEST-urz)
Investors are people who give money to a company so it can operate. In return, the company gives money back to the investors if it makes a profit. Both private investors and the government owned part of the national bank.

For Further INFORMATION

Web Sites

Visit our home page for lots of links about Henry Clay:
http://www.childsworld.com/links.html

Note to Parents, Teachers, and Librarians:
We routinely verify our Web links to make sure they're safe,
active sites—so encourage your readers to check them out!

Books

Collier, Christopher, and James Collier. *Slavery and the Coming of the Civil War, 1831–1861.* New York: Benchmark Books, 2000.

Marquette, Scott. *War of 1812.* Vero Beach, Fla.: Rourke Publishing, 2003.

Tibbits, Alison. *Henry Clay: From "War Hawk" to the "Great Compromiser."* Berkeley Heights, N.J.: Enslow Publishers, 2003.

Places to Visit or Contact

Ashland, the Henry Clay Estate
To see the place where Clay lived for most of his life
120 Sycamore Road
Lexington, KY 40502
859/266-8581
www.henryclay.org

The U.S. Capitol Historical Society
To learn more about the lawmaking process
200 Maryland Avenue, N.E.
Washington, DC 20002
202/543-8919

Index

About the Author

MICHAEL BURGAN IS A FREELANCE WRITER OF BOOKS FOR children and adults. A history graduate of the University of Connecticut, he has written more than 60 fiction and nonfiction children's books for various publishers. For adult audiences, he has written news articles, essays, and plays. Mr. Burgan is the recipient of an Edpress Award and belongs to the Society of Children's Book Writers and Illustrators.